Songs my Heart has Taught Me

Bob Chilcott

for SSA and piano

Vocal score

OXFORD
UNIVERSITY PRESS

OXFORD

UNIVERSITY PRESS

Great Clarendon Street, Oxford OX2 6DP,
United Kingdom

Oxford University Press is a department of the University of Oxford.
It furthers the University's objective of excellence in research, scholarship,
and education by publishing worldwide. Oxford is a registered trade mark of
Oxford University Press in the UK and in certain other countries

Original version first published 2021. This version first published 2022.

Impression: 1

ISBN 978-0-19-356290-5

Music and text origination by Katie Johnston
Printed in Great Britain on acid-free paper by
Halstan & Co. Ltd, Amersham, Bucks.

Contents

Composer's note

It was a privilege and an honour to be invited to write the Raymond Brock Memorial Commission for the ACDA National Conference in Dallas in 2021. I was asked to write something that embraced certain aspects of diversity: a rich, beautiful, and complex subject. I asked a brilliant young poet, Delphine Chalmers, to come on this journey with me to create this piece. As the National Conference ended up taking place virtually, this piece was first performed by the BBC Singers with pianist Anna Tilbrook, in a video recording to be broadcast to delegates. The piece was originally written for mixed voices, but some months later I re-worked it as this version for The Children's Chorus of Washington, D.C. and their Musical Director, Margaret Clark.

I have learnt so much from a life of extensive travel, through music and collaboration with many different people, but the overriding thing is that, as Maya Angelou says in her great poem 'Human Family', 'We are more alike, my friends, than we are unalike'. Throughout life, music has been my barometer; it has helped me to understand so many things and so many people, and I hold this deep in my heart, hence the title *Songs my Heart has Taught Me*. Delphine and I decided to use musical concepts as titles for the four songs that make up the work, exploring how these can help us to understand commonality.

The first song, 'Unison', is an anthem to unity that ends with the powerful line, 'The song of the future and the song of our souls are in unison'. 'Harmony', written in a more fluid, musical-theatre style, touches on people's need to be accepted, in a way like a note in a chord, in such a way that we can feel embraced, as Delphine writes so eloquently: 'In the song of shared acceptance lies an inner harmony'. The third song, 'Rhythm', is a spiky piece with a beat that tells of life's rhythm, of the pulse that the living all share, and it urges us to seize the day. Finally, in 'Resolution', the melody is spun by the singers over a simple, recurring chord structure. The poetic refrain is strongly influenced by the words of the 14th-century female mystic, Julian of Norwich: 'All shall be well, and all shall be well and all manner of thing shall be well'. The piece ends quietly and tonally, but of course does not completely resolve. That is the story of life.

Duration: *c*.11 minutes

Commissioned by the American Choral Directors Association as the 2021 Raymond W. Brock Memorial Commission.
This version is dedicated to Margaret Clark and the Children's Chorus of Washington, D.C.

Songs my Heart has Taught Me

Delphine Chalmers (b. 1998)

BOB CHILCOTT

1. Unison

Printed in Great Britain

OXFORD UNIVERSITY PRESS, MUSIC DEPARTMENT, GREAT CLARENDON STREET, OXFORD OX2 6DP

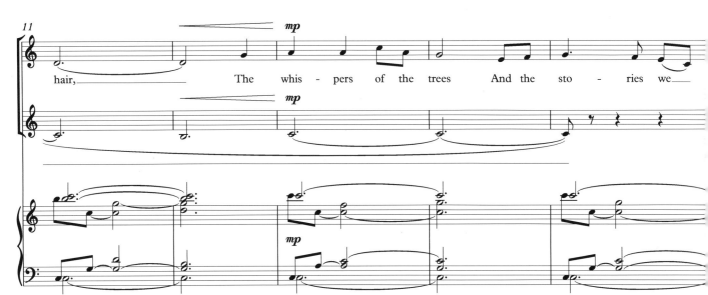

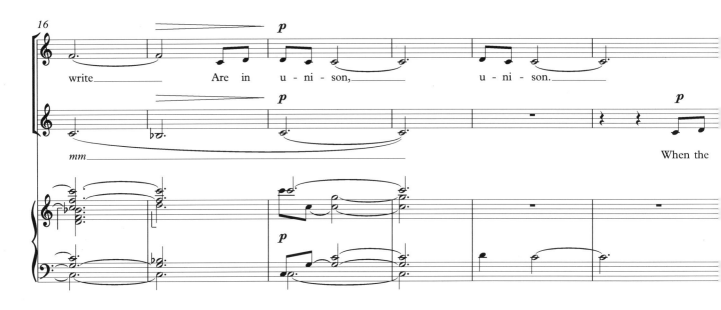

on new shores, The surge of the tides And the

press of a hand Are in u - ni - son,

u - ni - son. When the brav - est i - deals Take wing in soar - ing

u - ni - son. When the brav - est i - deals Take wing in soar - ing

flocks__ And make a home in warm - er__ skies,_____ The

flocks__ And make a home in warm - er skies,_____ The

pat - terns of the birds And the lives__ we weave_____ Are in

pat - terns of the birds And the lives we weave_____ Are in

u - ni - son,_____ u - ni - son._____

u - ni - son,_____ u - ni - son.

When dreams lin - ger in wak - ing thought Like teas - ing con - stel - la - tions And hope fills e - ven hope - less hearts, The song of the fu - ture And the song of our

2. Harmony

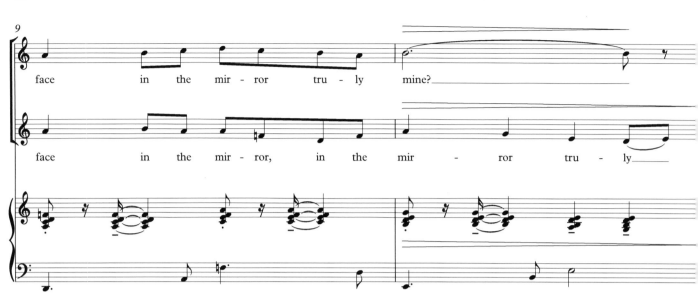

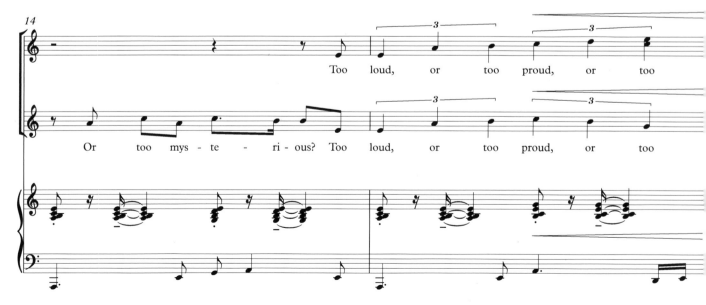

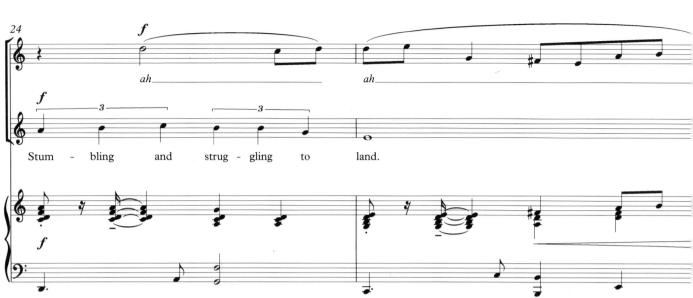

Stum - bling and strug - gling to land.

I can soar through it all. May - be it's

I can soar through it all. May - be it's

time for my last cur - tain call, my last cur - tain

time for my last cur - tain call, my last cur - tain

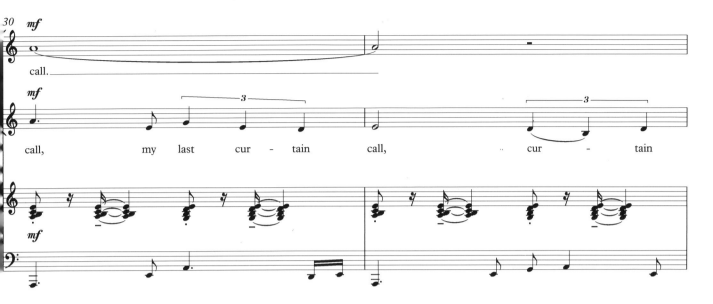

call.

call, my last cur - tain call, cur - tain

call.

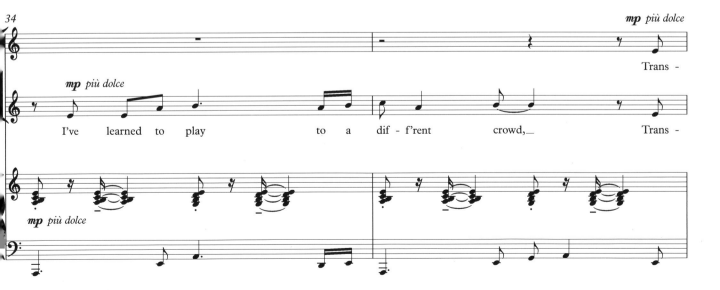

mp più dolce

Trans -

I've learned to play to a dif - f'rent crowd,___ Trans -

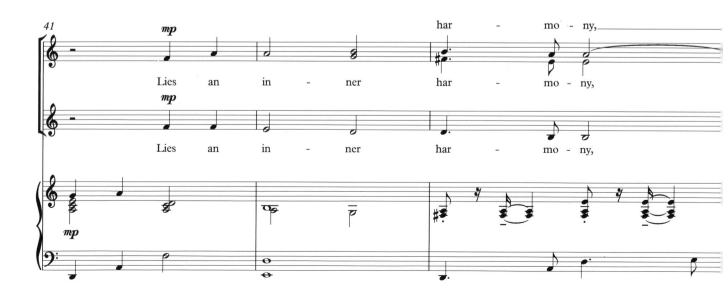

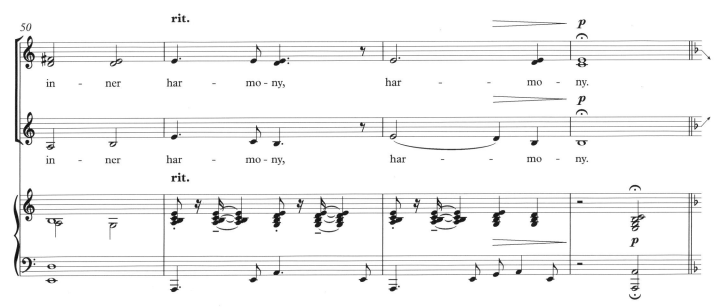

3. Rhythm

Clap it. Tap it. E - ven rap it. Feel the pulse and__ set life's beat.

S. 1
S. 2

unis.

Clap it. Tap it. E - ven rap it. Feel the pulse and__ set life's beat.

A.

Clap it. Tap it. E - ven rap it. Feel the pulse and__ set life's beat.

You can sense the

You can sense it in the swag-ger of a head-phoned guy when they

for Fern and Rob

4. Resolution

Calm and with great repose ♩ = c.63

TUTTI VOICES

My heart has taught me a song to sing in ev - 'ry lone - ly hour, though each pass - ing se - cond marks a mo - ment lost in time. The si - lence holds with - in it o - ther gifts._____ My youth hid - den in the beat - ing rain like

PIANO

p dolce

con Ped.

a tempo

Life has taught me a way to find the miss-ing chord I need, though mi - nor and ma - jor blend with-in my

me - mo - ry. The e - cho holds with - in it o - ther voi - ces. Love and

poco espress.

poco rit.

loss en - twined in a sin - gle note like hearts and i - ni - tials carved in oak. For all